NED KELLY

Copyright © 2023 by Aidan Phelan

All rights reserved. No part of this book may be reproduced in any manner whatsoever without written permission except in the case of brief quotations embodied in critical articles and reviews.

First Printing, 2023

ISBN: 978-0-6457001-4-5
ISBN (eBook): 978-0-6457001-5-2

Ned Kelly
The Bullet-Proof Bushranger

Aidan Phelan

Australian Bushranging

Dedicated to the future generations who will nurture and preserve our history, inspired by stories just like this one...

When Ned Kelly was a young boy, he rescued another boy, named Dick Shelton, from drowning.

Many years later, he wore the green sash he was given as a gift by Dick's grateful parents under a suit of bullet-proof armour.

By then, he had become Australia's most notorious outlaw...

1

A long time ago in Victoria, Australia, there was a family called the Kellys. There was Mrs. Kelly and her kids Annie, Ned, Maggie, Jim, Dan, Kate and Grace, and they lived in a little town called Greta.

Ellen Kelly had come from Ireland with her family as a girl. She married Ned's dad, John, when she was 18 years old.

The Kellys were very poor and sometimes they did criminal things to help them get by, such as stealing. In fact, The Kellys and their relatives, the Quinns and Lloyds, got into trouble so often that any time something went wrong in Greta the police thought it must have been them that did it. This made them feel like they were being picked on and bullied by the police.

Ned was the oldest boy in the family and when he was twelve years old his dad passed away, so it became Ned's responsibility to work and get money for his family. He did all sorts of chores on the farm like chopping wood and fixing the fences — very hard work for a kid!

One of the things Ned would do to get money was to find lost horses and cattle and hide them until someone offered a reward for them, then he would take them in and get the reward money. Sometimes the missing animals he brought in were not missing before he found them, but Ned thought that as long as nobody knew that bit, he could stay out of trouble.

Ned Kelly loved horses, even if they didn't belong to him.

Ned's uncles were friends with an infamous bushranger named Harry Power. But Harry was old and sick, and this made bushranging hard. The uncles said young Ned would be the perfect helper. So, when he was fifteen years old, Ned secretly became Harry Power's apprentice and had to cook the meals and tend the camp. He also had to feed the horses and clean up their poo. In return Harry would share what he stole with Ned and teach him all about being a bushranger.

Harry used to bail up people who were travelling on the roads around Beechworth and take any valuables they had. Sometimes, if they had no valuables, he would take anything he might think was useful. Once, when he stuck up a mail coach, he stole a quilt from a little boy who had been riding next to the driver. When Harry was robbing people, Ned usually stayed in the bush to hold the horses but occasionally Harry would let him join in on the robbing.

Unfortunately, Harry was a very cranky, grumpy, rude old bushranger who would treat Ned poorly, so he decided it was time to go home. The police arrested Ned because they believed that he had been helping Harry Power, but because nobody could prove it he was let go. However, the police now kept an eye on Ned, waiting for him to slip up and do something wrong so they could catch him.

Harry Power, the grumpiest bushranger in Victoria.

Ned became a very angry young man because he thought everyone was out to get him. Whenever a crime was committed near Greta, the police would try and pin it on Ned Kelly and his relatives. Then, when Harry Power was finally caught, lots of people thought Ned must have dobbed him in so they picked on him. He got into fights with all kinds of people and sometimes this got him into so much trouble he went to jail.

Harry Power had a peacock that he used as a guard dog.

When he was caught, the peacock was sheltering from the rain, so it didn't hear the police coming.

    The first time Ned went to jail was when he got into an argument with a travelling salesman named Jeremiah McCormack and his wife, who had accused him of pinching their horse to help a rival salesman get his wagon out of a bog. The bogged salesman had written a nasty letter to the McCormacks, who thought it had come from Ned. They got into an argument with Ned and he got so angry he punched Mr. McCormack in the face. Because of the punch and the note, Ned was sent to jail in Beechworth for half a year.

Ned was always up for a fight, even if it was against a policeman like Senior-Constable Hall!

One day he got into a fight with a policeman named Senior-Constable Edward Hall who thought Ned was riding on a stolen horse. The horse had been taken by a friend of the Kellys named "Wild" Wright, who told Ned he had lost her. When Ned found the horse, he decided to take her for a ride and show off to some of the local girls he fancied, and this was when Senior-Constable Hall tried to arrest him. Ned didn't want to co-operate, and it quickly became a wrestling match. The fight was very nasty, and Ned was hurt very badly when Hall hit him over the head with his revolver. He went to court and the judge sent Ned to jail for three years for receiving a stolen horse.

Ned was sent to Beechworth Gaol (the old-fashioned spelling of jail), then to Pentridge Prison and a prison hulk called *Sacramento* in Williamstown. Most of the work he did was breaking big rocks to be used for building, which was very hard work. It was very tough being in jail away from his family for three years, but Ned was so well behaved and such a hard worker he was allowed to get out a little bit early.

He decided he wanted to stay out of trouble, but first he wanted to settle the score with "Wild" Wright over that stolen horse. They had a boxing match and after twenty rounds Ned was declared the winner. He even had his photo taken in his boxing outfit to celebrate his win. After that fight, Ned and "Wild" became close friends.

Isaiah "Wild" Wright got his nickname because he was always getting into trouble, and didn't care much for rules.

In Ned's day, when you went to jail you had to wear an itchy, grey woollen uniform.

For the first few months of your sentence, you weren't allowed to talk, and had to wear a mask so that other prisoners couldn't see your face.

You were only allowed out of your cell for one hour a day to exercise by walking up and down a yard.

Ned Kelly's boxing outfit looks very strange compared to how boxers dress now. He wore his shorts over his undies, but undies were a lot bigger in 1874!

2

When Ned was out of jail, he did lots of jobs like chopping down trees and working at a sawmill, but he was still being picked on because of the trouble he had caused in the past. No matter what he did, that trouble always followed him. There was a rich farmer named James Whitty who had said Ned stole a bull from him, and Ned got so angry about this rumour that he decided to steal from Whitty and his friends for real to teach them a lesson.

James Whitty did not like Ned Kelly. He liked him even less when Ned started stealing his horses!

Ned teamed up with some of his friends and family and stole horses from everyone they felt had been picking on them. They sold them and made lots of money, but most importantly for them, they upset all the people who they thought deserved it. Of course, the police did not agree with this behaviour and looked all over for the culprits. Two of the men who had bought stolen horses from Ned were sent to jail for it, but the police never did catch the real thieves.

Ned Kelly blamed Constable Fitzpatrick for all of the bad things that happened after his visit to the Kelly house in April 1878.

One night, a policeman named Constable Alexander Fitzpatrick went to Mrs. Kelly's house to arrest Ned's 15-year-old brother Dan because he had heard that someone thought he had stolen some horses. Fitzpatrick had been Ned's friend for a while, but they fell out after he arrested Ned for being drunk and riding his horse on the footpath in Benalla.

Even though Dan agreed to go quietly so long as he was allowed to finish his dinner first, there was a fight and the policeman left with a sore head and an injured wrist. He said that Mrs. Kelly had hit him in the head with a shovel and Ned Kelly had shot him in the wrist and made him cut the bullet out with a knife.

The next day Mrs. Kelly was arrested, along with two men named William Skillion and William Williamson who Fitzpatrick said had been there with guns. However, Ned and Dan were not arrested because they had gone into the bush to hide from the police. While they were away Mrs. Kelly was sent to jail for three years for attacking Constable Fitzpatrick and the men were sent to jail for six years each.

Ned and Dan tried to strike a deal with the police to turn themselves in if their mum was released from jail, but they were ignored. This made the Kelly brothers furious.

Now it was just the Kelly sisters Kate and Grace and their little half-siblings alone on the farm to look after everything. Jim was in jail in New South Wales for stock theft, and Maggie was living on her own farm raising a family. The police spied on the farm to see if Ned and Dan would come back but they never caught them. There was a £100 reward for catching Ned, which was almost as much money as most people would make in a year in those days.

The Kellys lived in a small house made of wood and bark. They had to grow their own veggies in a little garden and had a pet kangaroo.

The Kelly hideout on Bullock Creek was not a very posh place to live.

Ned and Dan had gone to hide in the Wombat Ranges at Dan's hut on Bullock Creek, where they mined for gold and tried to make whiskey. They thought this way they could make some money to hire a lawyer to get their mum out of jail. They were helped by a lot of their friends and family like their cousin Tom Lloyd and Dan's mate Steve Hart, who was a jockey from Wangaratta. They worked together to build a second hut further up the creek using big logs and a steel door, so that if the police tried to catch them there, they would be safe in a shoot-out.

In October 1878, four policemen rode into the bush to catch the Kelly brothers. Their names were Constable Thomas Lonigan, Constable Michael Scanlan, Constable Thomas McIntyre and Sergeant Michael Kennedy. They rode the whole day before they decided to build a camp along Stringybark Creek but did not realise that Ned and Dan had been tracking them.

Sergeant Kennedy was from Mansfield Police Station. He was very respected in the community.

The police were very nervous because they had never met Ned Kelly, except for Constable Lonigan who had been in a fight with him the year before. They knew how dangerous Ned Kelly could be, and they were all on high alert.

Constable Scanlan was from Mooroopna Police Station. He was one of Sergeant Kennedy's best friends.

The next day Ned and Dan went to the police camp with their friends Steve Hart and Joe Byrne, who was a friend of theirs from the Woolshed Valley near Beechworth. They wanted to steal all the guns and supplies from the police and send them back home. When they got there, only Constable Lonigan and Constable McIntyre were at the camp. Ned told the police to bail up, but Lonigan ran and Ned shot him dead. Constable McIntyre was terrified but did exactly what he was told to do while the bushrangers robbed the camp and asked him questions. They even ate the dinner McIntyre had made for his mates. McIntyre tried to get Ned Kelly to agree not to hurt the other police, and Ned told him if he could get them to surrender then nobody else would be hurt.

When Constable Scanlan and Sergeant Kennedy came back for tea, Constable McIntyre tried to get them to surrender but there was a fight. Ned shot Scanlan and Kennedy dead as well. McIntyre managed to escape to tell everyone what had happened and get help, even though he was badly hurt when he was knocked off the horse that he was riding by a low tree branch as he was racing through the bush.

Constable Lonigan was from Violet Town Police Station. He was the only one on the team who knew Ned Kelly.

Constable Lonigan and Sergeant Kennedy had many children who now had to grow up without their dads, and Mrs. Lonigan and Mrs. Kennedy struggled to make ends meet without their husbands to bring in money from their jobs. Constable Scanlan had no family in Australia but had told one of his friends to look after his dog if he didn't come back alive.

A lot of people were very sad for the families of the dead men, and many more were angry about what had happened or scared that the Kellys might hurt them too. The government made a special new law that they thought would make it easier to catch the bushrangers, and they put out a reward of more than £2000 for their capture, dead or alive.

Constable McIntyre was also from Mansfield Police Station. If he had not escaped, nobody would have known what had happened to the police.

Ned Kelly and his gang were now officially outlaws, and they knew that the police would be out everywhere to catch them for such a terrible crime. They would have to rely on help from their family and friends, as well as their bush skills, to survive.

Ned Kelly emerged from the bush shouting, "Bail up! Throw up your arms," just like the bushrangers he had heard about when he was a young boy.

3

A couple of months later Ned and his gang stuck up a farm near a place called Faithfulls Creek and stayed there for the night. They locked everyone up in the tool shed, except for the women, and even stole new clothes from a travelling salesman so they would look respectable, instead of like bloodthirsty bushrangers. They also covered themselves with perfume so they would smell like flowers instead of horses and sweaty underarms. The next morning Ned, Joe and Steve cut down the telegraph wires to stop news about what they were up to reaching the police.

Ned Kelly tried to get into the bank with a fake cheque. When he got inside he bailed everyone up.

That afternoon, Ned, Steve and Dan rode into the town of Euroa. Joe stayed behind at Faithfulls Creek to guard the prisoners. Ned and Steve robbed the bank, while Dan guarded them, and they stole around £2000, which they later gave to their family and friends as a way to thank them for their help. They took everyone in the bank back to Faithfulls Creek, including the bank manager's wife, children and servants. In fact, there were so many extra people that they had to borrow a buggy to get them all there.

When they returned to the station, they relaxed with their prisoners and Ned told everyone his side of what happened to Constable Fitzpatrick and the police at Stringybark Creek. He said that Fitzpatrick had lied about being shot and that he only killed the police so they wouldn't shoot him. As they were leaving with their loot, Ned told everyone not to raise the alarm or he would come back and shoot them. They then showed off their horse-riding skills as they galloped off into the night.

The police were furious and started locking up anyone they thought was helping the bushrangers, but this didn't stop people trying to help Ned, Dan, Joe and Steve. In fact, some people were getting so angry about what the police were doing that it seemed like even more people were supporting the gang than before!

Ned's horse was a bay mare named Mirth.

There were reports in the newspapers all the time about the outlaws and a lot of people were scared that they could be robbed or killed by them at any time. They wanted the police to catch the bushrangers quickly so they would feel safe, but because the police did not know how to find them in the bush people started to get angry at them. To stop the gang from trying to rob another bank in Victoria, soldiers were sent to guard all the banks.

Superintendent Nicolson had been one of the troopers that captured Harry Power in 1870.

The man in charge of the hunt for the Kelly Gang was Superintendent Charles Nicolson, who had been one of the men that had caught Harry Power almost ten years earlier and had lots of experience hunting down bushrangers. He was a grouchy Scotsman who happened to be one of the best detectives in Victoria, but even he struggled to find any useful clues about where the gang were. Sometimes the information was too old, sometimes it was wrong or completely made up! Just after the bank robbery at Euroa, Nicolson became ill and had to retire from the hunt for a while.

When the money they had stolen ran out, the gang decided to go to New South Wales to get more. In February 1879, they stuck up the police in Jerilderie. They woke them up in the middle of the night, locked them up in a cell, still dressed in their pyjamas. For the next couple of days, they dressed in the police uniforms so they could disguise themselves as troopers sent to protect the town from bushrangers.

Steve Hart dressed as a New South Wales mounted trooper to help Ned scope out the town without being recognised.

The next morning some of the gang went into town in disguise to map out the telegraph and have their horses shod, which they put on the police expense account. That night Ned and Joe plotted how to rob the bank and put the finishing touches on a long letter Ned wanted to have published in the local newspaper, which he thought would tell everyone his side of the story and show that all the bad things he did were someone else's fault.

Even though Ned could read and write, he made Joe write his letter for him because he was better writer.

On the big day, the locals were rounded up and kept in the pub where they were guarded by Dan. Joe went next door and bailed up the bank, where he was joined by Ned and Steve.

When they went to open the safe, they found out that they needed the manager's key. Joe said they should smash it open with a sledgehammer, but Ned sent Steve to find the key instead. It wasn't long before Steve found the bank manager who was in the middle of having a bath while the bank was being robbed! The gang stole thousands of pounds in cash, gold and valuables. Ned also destroyed bank documents that he thought would stop the bank from forcing poor farmers to pay them money that they owed.

While they were in the bank, some men came in to see what was happening. One of them was the local schoolteacher, who Ned told to let the students have the day off in honour of the gang's visit to town. Afterwards, Joe destroyed the telegraph and Ned gave a big speech in the pub to all the prisoners and gave his letter to the bank accountant for safekeeping. The newspaper editor had seen that Ned was robbing the bank and ran out of town in fear, so that meant Ned had to trust someone else to make sure the letter was published after he had gone.

Superintendent Hare was almost two metres tall, which was huge in the 1870s. Sadly for him, basketball had not been invented yet.

The reward for the gang was raised to £8000, which was an incredible amount! The man who was now in charge of the hunt for the outlaws was Superintendent Francis Hare, who was a very tall man with a big, bushy beard who had come to Australia from South Africa. He had a lot of experience catching criminals and was another one of the police who had caught Harry Power. He thought that by going out and searching in the bush they could find the outlaws.

He also began to receive information from a close friend of the gang's named Aaron Sherritt. Hare liked Sherritt so much that he followed all of his suggestions on how to catch the gang, like sending troopers to spy on Joe's mum's house. What Hare didn't realise was that Aaron was giving the police bad information to keep them distracted while the gang moved around.

Because the search parties were not able to find any trace of the outlaws, a team of special Aboriginal trackers were brought down from Queensland to find the gang. Even though they were incredible at tracking people in the bush, far better than the other police, even they found it hard to locate the outlaws. Still, Ned was terrified of them and called them, "little devils".

Sub-Inspector Stanhope O'Connor and his Native Police came all the way from K'gari (Fraser Island) to track the outlaws.

The Jerilderie letter is 56 pages long.

In the letter Ned says a lot of nasty things about the police, and calls them...

"...big, ugly, fat-necked, wombat-headed, big-bellied, magpie-legged, narrow-hipped, splaw-footed sons of Irish bailiffs, or English landlords..."

4

Tom Lloyd was Ned's cousin and his best friend.

While the police were trying to find the outlaws in the bush, the friends and family of the gang were keeping them safe. Ned's sister Maggie and his cousin Tom Lloyd would bring them food, fresh clothing, ammunition for their weapons and newspapers so that they knew what was going on. Tom would also escort the gang when they were travelling from place to place, and there were people who thought he was like a fifth member of the gang.

Maggie Kelly was married to William Skillion, who had been sent to jail for the attack on Constable Fitzpatrick.

Maggie had even more responsibility than Tom because she was looking after her own family, helping Kate at their mum's house, and regularly getting supplies to her brothers while trying to avoid being caught by police. Maggie was an excellent horse-rider and just as daring as her brothers. She would sometimes trick police into chasing her as a distraction so that they didn't find the secret meeting points. Without supporters like Maggie and Tom, Ned and his gang would not have survived nearly as long as they had in the bush.

Aaron Sherritt and Joe Byrne grew up together in the Woolshed Valley.

Meanwhile, Aaron Sherritt was still being paid for his information even though it was never helpful. Where he told the police to keep watch at Mrs. Byrne's house was a spot where they wouldn't be able to see Joe coming home to visit his mum and get supplies. Every night, when he went there with the police, he would tell them that this was night they would finally catch the outlaws, but they never did.

Unfortunately, some of Ned's supporters thought Aaron really was dobbing on the gang and told the bushrangers to shoot him before he got them captured or killed. Joe wrote to Aaron, who had been his best friend since they were little boys, to warn him that people suspected him of betraying the gang, but this did not stop Aaron.

Ned decided it was time to do something really dramatic to stop the police chasing him once and for all. There had been bushranging in Australia for almost one hundred years, but in all that time nobody had figured out how to protect themselves from being shot, but now Ned Kelly had discovered how to turn himself into a bullet-proof bushranger. The gang made themselves suits of armour out of plough mouldboards, which were heavy plates of iron. Some of the metal was stolen, some of it was donated, and it took them months to make these suits to protect them from the police. All four of the gang members had their own suit of armour.

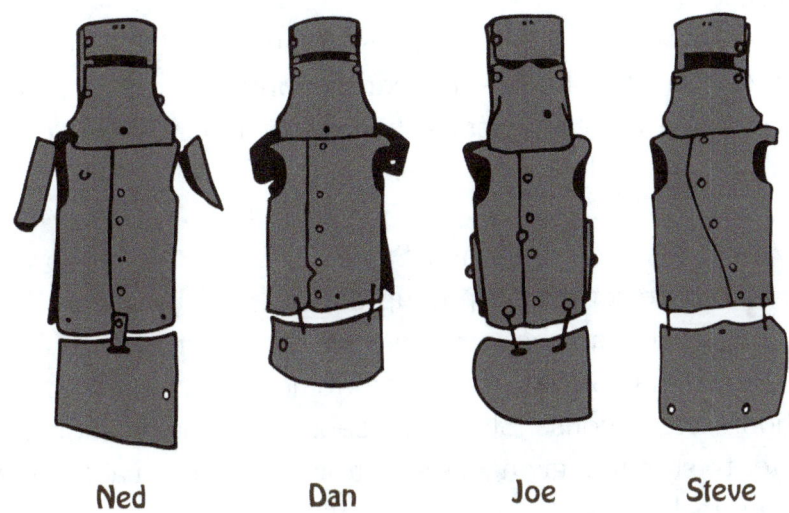

Ned   **Dan**   **Joe**   **Steve**

It was decided that on a Saturday night they would shoot Aaron Sherritt for his betrayal, just like they had been told to do by their supporters. This would make the police rush out on a special train to find out what had happened. The gang would break the railway line, and this would make the train crash, taking out all the troopers and trackers that had been chasing them. The spot where they chose to break the tracks was at a town called Glenrowan.

Aaron Sherritt lived in a tiny hut near Beechworth at a place called Devil's Elbow.

On a gloomy winter night in June 1880, Joe and Dan kidnapped a German man named Anton Wick, who was Aaron Sherritt's neighbour. They went to Aaron's hut and made Anton knock on the door and pretend he was lost. When Aaron answered the door, Joe shot him dead.

There were four policemen in the hut, and they were so terrified that they hid in the bedroom until the morning and forced Aaron's wife and her mother to stay under the bed, even after the outlaws had gone away.

Meanwhile, Ned Kelly and Steve Hart were in Glenrowan and had made some men pull up the train tracks. When Dan and Joe arrived, all the men were kept prisoner in the Glenrowan Inn while Steve guarded the women and children in the stationmaster's house. Steve also kept an eye on the stationmaster to stop him giving a signal to warn the train about the broken track.

Because it took such a long time for the police in town to find out about poor Aaron, Ned's plan failed. All day they kept taking more and more prisoners to stop anyone spoiling their trap. The prisoners began getting bored, so Dan suggested having sports games and dances.

The Glenrowan Inn was run by a woman named Ann Jones. She lived there with her children, who all helped her operate the business.

One of the prisoners was the local schoolteacher, whose name was Thomas Curnow. When he heard about Ned's horrible plan to hurt and kill the people on the special train and decided he was going to stop him. All day he tried to do favours for Ned and convince him he was on his side so that he could avoid suspicion. In the evening he asked Ned to let him take his family home and Ned let him go because he had been so helpful all day. He told Curnow, "go straight to bed and don't dream too loud!"

What Ned didn't realise was that Curnow lived very close to the railway, so when he heard the train was coming, he went out with a red scarf and a candle to use as a danger signal. When the engine stopped, he told the train driver about what Ned had done to the tracks and the police safely arrived at the train station.

Thomas Curnow used his sister's red llama-wool scarf and a candle as a danger signal for the police train.

5

The local policeman from Glenrowan, Constable Hugh Bracken, had managed to sneak out and told the police that the bushrangers were in the pub. The police, led by Superintendent Hare, rushed over and took aim. The gang were already waiting for them on the veranda, dressed in their suits of bullet-proof armour, and started shooting. The police fired back, and the prisoners could be heard screaming in the inn as bullets whizzed around them.

Dan Kelly had only had his 19th birthday a few weeks before the Glenrowan siege.

Superintendent Hare was shot in the wrist and had to be rushed to a doctor even though he tried to keep fighting. Although bullets bounced off the gang's armour, Ned and Joe were still injured because it only covered their heads and bodies. Joe was shot in the leg and could not walk, and Ned was shot in his foot and left arm. When the gang ran out of bullets they went around to the back of the inn.

Inside, a twelve-year-old boy named Johnny Jones, who was the son of the woman that ran the Glenrowan Inn, was shot by a police bullet. A man named Jack McHugh carried him to safety, even though he was almost shot too. An old man named Martin Cherry was shot by a police bullet as well, but he could not get out of the inn, so the other prisoners helped him lay in the kitchen where it was safe. It was a disaster!

Ned decided he had to find a way to escape but when he went out into the bush he passed out because of his injuries. Joe had stayed behind because he could only crawl around due to his broken leg, and Dan and Steve had been busy in the inn fighting the police when Ned left.

Superintendent John Sadleir took over for Hare at Glenrowan after he was injured.

The prisoners tried to run out of the inn, but the police shot at them because it was too dark to see who they were. Dan Kelly yelled out to the police to stop shooting so that the civilians could leave, but the police refused to stop. However, they did start aiming higher so they wouldn't hit anyone lying on the floor.

Over the next few hours, police reinforcements arrived in Glenrowan to help fight the outlaws. A party led by Sergeant Steele came from Wangaratta, and another came from Benalla with Superintendent Sadleir.

Joe Byrne's last words were a toast to his friends, "Here's to many more days in the bush, boys!"

As the battle continued Joe was shot dead while having a drink at the bar, and a nineteen-year-old boy named Michael Reardon was shot in the back by Sergeant Steele when he was trying to get his three-year-old brother to safety. Luckily, he survived, but he was badly hurt. Some of the women and children managed to escape with Ann Jones and her teenage daughter Jane leading them by candlelight through the battlefield.

In the early morning Ned appeared behind the police, but because of the thick fog some of the police thought he must have been a bunyip or the devil because all they could see was a big, scary shadow that was bulletproof and shouting at them. Sergeant Steele realised that it was Ned Kelly and that his armour didn't protect his legs, so he fired his gun at Ned's knee and brought him down. Ned was captured alive but badly wounded and taken to safety.

Even though Ned was badly hurt, he still managed to fight the police while wearing his full suit of armour, which weighed around 40kg.

Sergeant Arthur Steele was a friend of Sergeant Kennedy and had sworn to be at Ned Kelly's death or capture.

By the afternoon, all of the prisoners had been released from the inn. Sometime after this, Dan and Steve also died but nobody ever found out how. At the end of the battle the police burned the inn down and that was the end of the Kelly Gang, once and for all.

Dan and Steve were given to their families to be buried, but the police refused to give Joe Byrne to his friends, and he was buried in an unmarked grave in Benalla.

Ned Kelly was taken to Melbourne to recover from his injuries. He was said to have had close to 30 wounds from his final battle and it took him months to be well enough to go to trial.

When he was well enough, Ned was put on trial in Melbourne for the murder of Constable Lonigan and found guilty. Judge Redmond Barry sentenced him to be hanged to death.

Ned's friends and family tried to get the death sentence changed by getting people to sign a petition and having protests in the city, but it was decided that a hanging was the only way to punish Ned Kelly for his crimes.

Sir Redmond Barry was one of the top judges in Australia. In his time he had sent many bushrangers to jail.

Ned was allowed to see his family one last time and on November 11, 1880, he was hanged in Old Melbourne Gaol. Some said his last words were, "such is life."

The day before he was hanged, Ned Kelly had photos taken for his family.

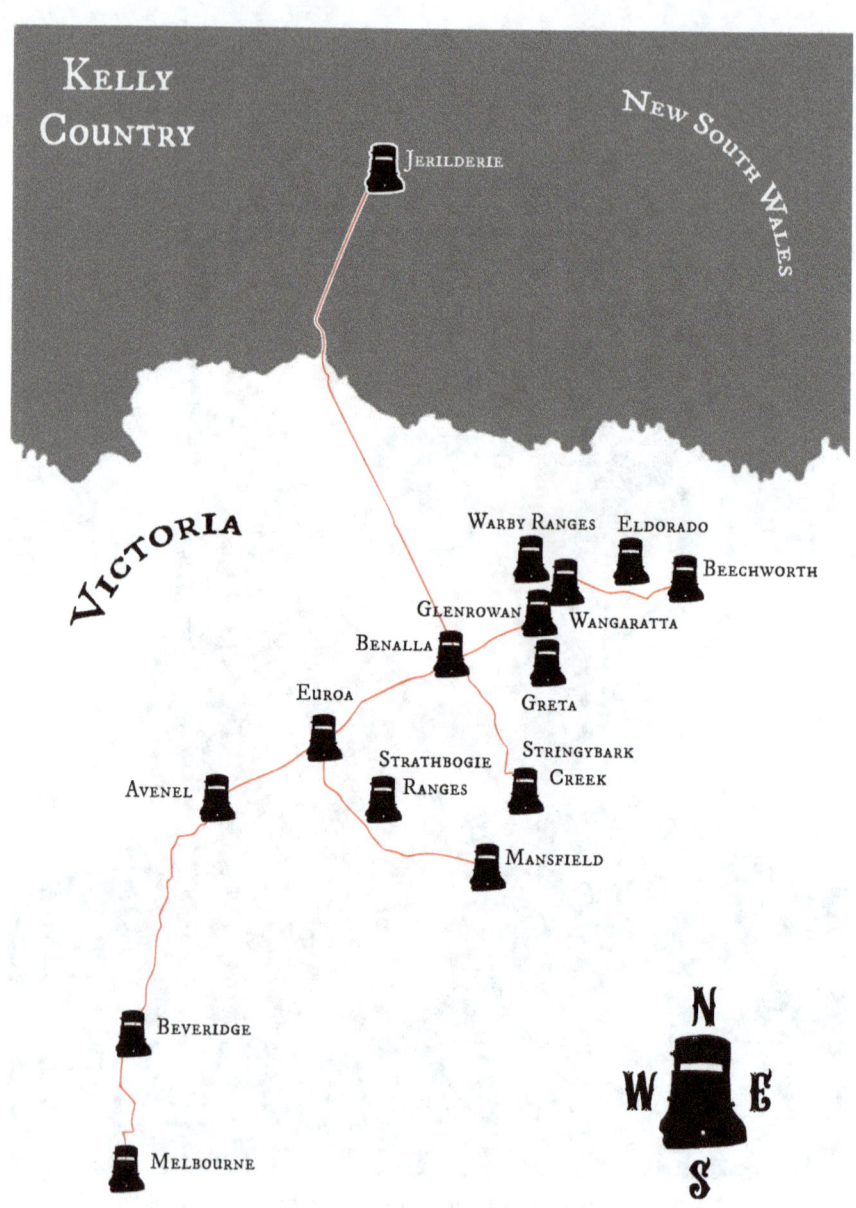

PLACES TO VISIT

Old Melbourne Gaol: This is where Ned Kelly was hanged, and his mother spent most of her prison sentence. There are many items on display related to Ned including his death mask, one of his revolvers and part of the scarf Thomas Curnow used to stop the police train.

State Library of Victoria, Melbourne: The state library was founded by Redmond Barry, the judge who sentenced Ned to death, because he believed everyone should have access to knowledge and education. The library has the largest collection of original images and documents related to the Kelly story, including the Jerilderie letter. They also have Ned Kelly's armour and one of his boots on display.

Victoria Police Museum, Melbourne: The Victoria Police have many fascinating objects on display, including a small number of the Kelly items in their collection. You can see Dan Kelly's and Steve Hart's armour as well as a bag wore Ned Kelly at Glenrowan.

The Kelly House, Beveridge: In Beveridge you can see a house that was built by Ned's father, Red Kelly, when the family lived in the village. It has recently been restored and landscaped.

Benalla Costume and Kelly Museum: The prized items in the collection of this museum include Ned's green silk sash, which he wore at Glenrowan and is said to have been given to him by the Shelton family after he rescued their son Richard from drowning, as well as an exact replica of Joe Byrne's armour. There are also the doors from the old Benalla lock-up as well as some smaller items believed to be connected to Ned Kelly.

Ned Kelly Discovery Hub, Glenrowan: This new, state-of-the-art facility introduces visitors to the Kelly story and the events of the Glenrowan siege. There are information panels, video presentations and a rooftop lookout.

Kellyland Glenrowan: This animated theatre and museum uses special effects, full scale dioramas and animatronics to take visitors back in time to the siege. The museum is full of unique items connected to local history, as well as the Kelly Gang and Victoria Police, such as firearms and police uniforms.

Kate's Cottage and Ned Kelly Museum, Glenrowan: The centrepiece of this attraction is a full scale, fully furnished replica of the Kelly house in Greta. There is also a museum which tells the Kelly story and shows many of the tools and equipment the Kelly family would have used around their home.

Beechworth Courthouse: This is where many of Ned's friends and family stood trial. The new upgrade scheduled to open in late 2023 will use audio visual displays to tell the stories of some of these trials.

Beechworth Gaol: This is where the Kellys and their associates spent time after committing crimes. Tours are frequently conducted through the site.

The Old Printery, Jerilderie: This is where Ned wanted his famous letter to be printed by the local newspaper editor. There are replica suits of the gang's armour on display and an exhibition about some of the local bushrangers. Afterwards, if you go on a stroll through town you will spot many of the buildings associated with the gang's visit there in 1879.

A NOTE TO PARENTS

This book is derived from factual information about the life story of Ned Kelly. He is a historical figure that many children find fascinating, but there are very few ways for them to learn his story in an age appropriate way. This is my attempt to cater to that need.

Unfortunately, it is impossible to tell this story without mentioning murder and robbery, as these were the very things that made Ned and his gang so notorious. I have done my best to address these in a gentle manner that such young people can understand. I encourage you to have a discussion with your young ones about what these things mean and why many people look at Ned Kelly as a villain because of them.

This story may raise some complex questions — children are far more insightful than we adults often give them credit for — so don't be afraid to respond to these, they're exactly the sort of questions stories like this should be raising. Ned's story is not one-dimensional and it's important for children to interrogate the ambiguities and the moral grey areas so that they can develop their own understanding of these concepts. These questions are a positive thing and if you can take the time to discuss them with your children you will be doing them a great benefit.

This text is aimed at primary school students and should be appropriate for most ages depending on their reading and comprehension skills. As a parent you are most equipped to know if this book is appropriate for your young reader, and I know you will make the right choice.

- *Aidan Phelan*

The real Ned Kelly, photographed the day before his execution in 1880.

BIBLIOGRAPHY

In all my years reading about Ned Kelly I have read so many books, news articles and historical documents that I've lost count. What I have listed here are just some of the books that I found most useful in my research over the years. I am sure that you will find them useful too. – Aidan Phelan

Jones, Ian, *Ned Kelly: A short life*. Second Edition. Hachette Australia, Sydney, New South Wales, 2003.

Molony, John N., *Ned Kelly*. Penguin Books, Melbourne, Victoria, 1989.

FitzSimons, Peter, *Ned Kelly: the story of Australia's most notorious legend*. Random House Australia, North Sydney, New South Wales, 2013.

Castles, Alex C. and Castles, Jennifer, *Ned Kelly's last days: setting the record straight on the death of an outlaw*. Allen and Unwin, Crow's Nest, New South Wales, 2005.

McMenomy, Keith *Ned Kelly: the authentic illustrated history*. Hardie Grant Books, South Yarra, Victoria, 2001.

Toohill, Trudy, (editor of compilation.) *The reporting of Ned Kelly & the Kelly gang*. Boolarong Press, Salisbury, Qld, 2015.

Brown, Max, *Ned Kelly: Australian son*. Georgian House, Melbourne, Victoria, 1948.

Kelly, Ned & McDermott, Alex, (writer of introduction.) *The Jerilderie Letter*. The Text Publishing Company, Melbourne, Victoria, 2001.

Kieza, Grantlee, *Mrs Kelly: The astonishing life of Ned Kelly's mother*. Harper Collins Publishers, Sydney, New South Wales, 2017.

Passey, Kevin J., *In search of Ned: a travelogue of Kelly country*. Lachlan Publishing, Albury, New South Wales, 1988.

Aidan Phelan is the writer and historian for *A Guide to Australian Bushranging*, an online resource that has been bringing Australia's outlaw heritage to a worldwide audience since 2017. His first novel for adults, *Glenrowan*, depicted the events leading to the capture and execution of Ned Kelly and has sold hundreds of copies around the world.

He is a self-taught illustrator who learnt how to draw by practicing and studying everything from comic books and cartoons to the works of artists like Norman Lindsay and Sir John Tenniel. He has contributed illustrations for several publications, including the book series *An Outlaw's Journal* and Judy Lawson's *The Clarke Bushrangers: A Clash of Cultures*.

Aidan has a Bachelor of Arts and a Diploma of Education, and studied writing and editing at what is now known as Melbourne Polytechnic. He was born and raised in the suburbs of Melbourne and developed a fascination with the story of Ned Kelly on his first visit to Glenrowan as a child. This soon grew to be a consuming passion for Australian history, culminating in the creation of *A Guide to Australian Bushranging* and the many books and related projects that he has worked on since then.

www.ingramcontent.com/pod-product-compliance
Lightning Source LLC
Chambersburg PA
CBHW050322010526
44107CB00055B/2351